New Stomach Old brain

HOW TO LOSE 125 POUNDS IN ONE YEAR
AND STAY SANE

Limor Haim Matityahoo (Limitz)

Graphic design: Limitz
Editing and Proofreading: Natalie Shochat
Photograph (before): Dudu Bistrov
Photographs (after): Studio Adigital
Publisher: Limitz

Website: www.NewStomacheOldBrain.co.il
Facebook: www.facebook.com/NewStomacheOldBrain
E-mail: newstomacheoldbrain@gmail.com

ISBN-13: 978-1540541086
ISBN-10: 1540541088

Contents

Thank you

To my beloved family

Thank you for your endless support of my choices, for always being there for me, and for the feeling of security you give me. Thanks to you, I am able to grow and develop myself in any direction I choose. To my wise mother, to my supporting father and to my one and only brother, for standing by me, always ready to give a hand, for your stability and endless encouragement. To my wonderful children Libi and Matan, who are my partners and friends for this journey of growing up together.

To my friends and community

Thank you for your openness, your support and endless curiosity, for your questions (and answers) about what you see. You have enabled me to observe life after weight loss surgery with curiosity and criticism. Thanks to you, I have written a book that will hopefully help those who are considering similar surgery, those who have already undergone it and their friends, to understand the mental impact that this operation causes, which is as strong as the external change in appearance.

Special thanks to my friends at "The Golden Group" that have accompanied me for years, to my friends in TR, to Amos and the "Bike the Way" group, to Hila, Yael, Nurit and Sela, for your unconditional support at difficult moments; to Haim, Nadav and Ayana and the "Weight losers" I have met along the way who shared their insights with me and let me share mine in return, to Ofira Shaul, Rivi Shachar, Dr. Goitein and the staff of Assuta Hospital, who introduced me to my new self.

To Yafit

Thank you for your support and friendship along the path we have shared. I am happy for you for finding the special road in your life, and I am full of love and respect for you.

Between You and Me

This book is about my **personal journey**, and it is not to be seen as a recommendation for any diet, operation or weight-loss practice for any person, fat or thin. It aims to show different aspects of **post-bariatric (weight loss) surgery life** and to give those who have not gone through it a glimpse of what life after it looks like. For all of you interested in this procedure I hope to offer new and even surprising insights about the thoughts running through the mind of an operated individual.

The book is based on my experience, and it presents different situations that came up during and after the operation, in the form of short stories. It also displays common situations and reactions by family and friends. I am not a doctor, psychologist or medical professional, and so I chose to share my insights based only on my personal experience and the accumulated experience of other weight losers I met along my journey.

This book doesn't recommend weight loss surgery. It also doesn't guarantee success for whoever chooses to go through it, or that she will have the same experiences that I have had. This operation, like any other operation, is a medical procedure. No one can predict how things will go and what the consequences will be.

The ability of each and every one to cope with the results of the operation, both physically and mentally, is individual and depends on one's personality and life experience.

In this book you'll find my thoughts and memories written soon after the operation and for the next two and a half years, as well as ideas and exercises that all aim at one purpose—to let a person who hasn't had this operation consider carefully if this is really what she wants, to get the feel of life with a stomach the size of a small banana.

The book unfolds gradually from the pre-surgery stage to life several years afterward. I do hope that this format will enable you to get a full view of this experience.

If you are after a weight loss surgery, I hope this book will help you in coping and recovering, and will encourage you to make the most from the new starting point you are at.

I'd like to thank you for reading the book, and look eagerly to read what you felt during and after reading it (I shared some links in the books first pages). If you feel it has helped you, I'll be glad if you'll recommend it to others so that they can also benefit from it.

Wishing you success in the choices of your life.

Yours,
Limor Haim Matityahoo (Limitz), July 2015

About the Author

My name is Limor Haim Matityahoo, and I am an internet savvy. I've been blogging and sharing my interests and experience regarding creativity, motherhood, design, entrepreneurship, business and marketing with my followers online since 2007. I graduated in 1996 from "Shenkar College of Textile and Fashion Design" in Tel Aviv with a Bsc degree, and a few years later I studied at the "Technion Institute" in Haifa for my Msc in Industrial Design. A few years after, I got married, had two children and got divorced.

I am known online by the nickname "Limitz" and I am the CEO, founder and owner of "Limitz – the Online Center of Marketing for Designers on ETSY" at www.limitz.co.il where I teach online marketing classes and give lectures for designers who wish to sell online. You can find my ebooks in English at limitz.etsy.com.

I also work as a Digital Marketing Coordinator in the high-tech industry at a global finance company.

Since my childhood, I have gone through an endless number of diet programs of all kinds, including weight watchers and sport programs. In each of these sessions, I lost between 20-40 lbs, regaining them soon after. My first record weight gain was during my army service in the Israeli Defense Force, in which I received officer ranks on my shoulders and an additional 66 lbs around my waist. The second record gain was twenty years later, during and after my pregnancies, which added another 66 lbs to my body.

On February 19, 2013, at the age of 41.5, I weighed 285 lbs extending over 5.6" (167 cms). On that very day, I entered the operating room and had a weight loss surgery known as "Laparoscopic Sleeve Gastrectomy (LSG)" or "the sleeve" operation. As a result of the operation, I lost 125 lbs during a period of a year and a half.

Apparently, the physical weight loss was the easier part of the process. Coping emotionally with the physical change was an inseparable part of it; an emotional confrontation that combined my feelings towards my body, the reaction of those around me and the endless interaction between them. This interaction accompanies me to this very day, years after the operation.

As a woman distinctly aware of beauty and esthetics, I was taken by surprise by the intensity of the reactions to my weight loss. I chose to embrace them wholeheartedly and examine the comments with curiosity and love.

Being a counselor and mentor for women, I had many opportunities to take an active part in conversations and discussions about female empowerment, weight and body image, and the general feelings women (and men) have regarding them.

I am an influential figure among women in Israel. I am exposed to new trends and styles in fashion and apparel; I wear mainly Israeli fashion and accessories and display them with pride and joy. These circumstances as a well-known figure among artists and designers, as well as a strong presence in the circles of stay-at-home moms, have influenced me to write this book.

I hope that this book enables those considering weight loss surgery and their family and friends to take a glimpse into a hidden world, a kind of matching inner world that doesn't necessarily resemble what we see from the outside, and understand **what it really means to live in a new body when your brain and habits stay behind with your old self.**

About the Book

I've been living with this new body of mine for about two and a half years, but even now when I walk down the street or in the shopping mall, I don't always recognize my reflection in the display window. Lately, I've been getting used to the idea that the reflection is me, and have started to like what I see. But I still don't turn around when someone calls out, "Hey, you really look great!"

Ever since my operation, I've received loads of compliments and flattering reactions. I'm surrounded by friends, family and colleagues, all very positive and supportive. I have no doubt at all of their best intentions. For most, I just say thanks and listen curiously to each and every remark.

These remarks were overwhelming to me, so I recorded them in my mind and then on paper. As a longtime blogger, I knew that everything I'd gone through from the moment I decided to have surgery was meant to be shared. I did actually write here and there about my experiences during that period; even though I'm not the superstitious type, I found myself walking around with a red string chain on my wrist (to ward off the evil eye) and hesitant to share my feelings too much with others. Now that my body feels stable I've reached the point where I feel I am able to share what I've been through because there is something very unique about carrying a fat mind in a thin body.

Weight loss surgery is not brain surgery. Although the weight loss patient usually loses dozens of pounds in a year, her habits and daily way of living do not change at the same rate. The major weight loss is accompanied by a challenging emotional adjustment that doesn't necessarily fit the new look.

This emotional challenge results in a mixture of positive social pressure combined with **increased exposure and an invasion of privacy** that can be very uncomfortable for those who prefer less exposure. It also involves **a physical adjustment to a different way of eating**, a struggle between **the will to eat** versus physical **inability** to do so—and a disturbing fear of being fat again.

This book is about all these challenges.

Since my operation, my mind has been overloaded with thoughts. Life after this special surgery adds an additional dose of questions, answers, and insights.

In this book, I would like to share with you, new understandings I've gained about weight loss surgery. Whether you've only heard about the operation, you're planning on having it, you've gone through it, or you know people who have had the operation, I'd like to give you a peek into the life of formerly obese people who, within a year, went through a huge change in their lives.

We're all human, and we're all equal, but part of us, a part that is **growing in relation to the general population**, have a stomach as big as a banana.

I have a **lot of criticism towards myself and towards the society** we have become. We have created a society that glorifies beauty and frowns at the lack of it; a society that decides who has good looks, and therefore decides that one is surely happy if her looks follow specific standards; a society that rarely accepts people who are different, either because of their looks or their behavior. Regretfully I say that we, as women and mothers, go along with this quite readily.

I'm not a feminist, but I'm a mother, a career woman and I am said to be an intelligent person, and I don't want my children to learn to judge others just because their looks don't match the accepted standards of beauty and fashion.

I really hope that this book will enable candidates for weight loss surgery and their families, before, during and after the operation, to realize that **the lbs that are lost are not a promise for lasting happiness**. I'd like to help them understand that the new thin people that surround them remained the same, they've just been given the opportunity to make a change in their life and that they might *not* know how to make the most of it.

In this book, I am sharing with you several short stories that present situations in which I was involved and that I have recorded since the operation. I hope these stories will allow a more compassionate and approving view of people whether they are fat or thin.

Why telling my story has become an important mission for me?

If you're reading this book, you may be considering undergoing weight loss surgery in order to lose weight, or have already undergone it, or you may know someone who has had it. Publishing this book is a moment of pure joy for me, and I feel like I'm on a mission.

From the moment I decided to have the operation, I became aware of a phenomenon that was just a tiny bit of what was to become a huge emotional wave right after the operation—**an enormous amount of empathy** that I am so thankful for, warm reactions and insights of those I met all along the way, even from those who weren't close friends.

This meant I became the center of attention, which was sometimes nice, but when this happened when all I wanted was to be left alone with my thoughts—it became challenging. So that's why I wrote this book. If I can make things easier, even a bit, for those who have decided to go through this procedure, then I've done my part.

The physical result of the operation is quite obvious, but the emotional and social changes experienced by the weight loser are not common knowledge.

Our culture idolizes the perfect, thin body and worships diets of any kind; so obviously, a person who loses a large amount of weight, and in such a short time, **attracts public attention**. Not everyone can stand this intense interest. Some people are used to being in the corner, behind the curtains, some choose to stay in the shadows whereas some (and there are a few) are natural party centers who love attention at all times.

When substantial weight loss occurs, the new look draws **positive attention** that suddenly transforms you into a pretty, admired and popular person, and this is a new one, something that the majority of obese people have never faced before.

This book is all about the new perspective that you, your (new) body and your (old) mind go through after the surgery. In it, you will find my point of view as well as incidents and a glimpse of my everyday life after the operation. I also include exercises that aim to help you understand what a person goes through from the moment the operation is over—as far as emotions and eating habits are concerned.

I have no doubt that friends of those who have had weight loss surgery, as well as those who will be undergoing it in the near future, will benefit from the book and will get a true understanding of the dramatic change in the lives of weight losers. For those about to have surgery, I hope the book will help reduce their uncertainty and enable their relatives and friends to understand them better.

I hope you enjoy reading the book. If you are having surgery soon, I wish you lots of success, and I recommend sharing the book with your closest ones—family and friends. I hope this book will help you live your new life after the operation in **good physical and mental health**, with the cooperation and understanding of your dear ones.

Life before the operation

We are so influenced by myths. From the day we are born we are taught right from wrong, true and false, beautiful from ugly. We have all grown up hearing certain "truths" repeated over and over by influential figures that have an opinion about every topic in the world including good looks and proper nutrition. This brainwashing is so common in our society that most of us don't ever stop to wonder if this even makes sense.

In this chapter, I would like to present some popular myths that deal with obesity, thinness, and dieting— and **shatter them**.

1. Diets don't work!

After years of struggling with my weight, I learned that:

- I like what I see in the mirror, and that's a lot more important than whatever anybody else thinks.
- Diets only cause you to gain weight.

This brought me to one conclusion:

There must be another way. And if there is another way, I'll find it, no matter what. After realizing that the brainwashing I've undergone in my life, dozens of diets and a general feeling of dissatisfaction aren't leading me to a happier and healthier body, **I quit.** I refused to drive my body crazy again. I didn't want to do more harm than I had already done. I refused to listen to the people around me who insisted that I needed a diet, that I didn't look good, and that I must "do something" with myself. What I understood the best was that **diets are not the solution for losing weight**, and I mean long-term weight loss, not just for a few weeks or months.

There were times when I didn't like the way I looked, and there were times when I was pleased with myself. I didn't ever mind having a "large behind," I loved myself, I went out on dates and I was popular. My studies and my great job completely fulfilled me.

There were 2 periods in my life in which I gained A LOT of weight. During my 2.5 years of service in the IDF, I gained 67 lbs. That was in my early 20s. The next period was in my 30s—I married at the age of 31, and my two children were born. During the three years of pregnancies and childbirth, I gained another 67 lbs. At this point, I was defined as OBESE with an excess of 120-140 lbs.

My children's father never criticized me about what I ate, and he never judged me for my looks or my body. When I reached the peak of over 265 lbs, I remember that he gently suggested I take care of myself, for the sake of my health and for the children. But I was firm about never going on diets anymore. My past experiences had shown me the results of starving my body, and since I hadn't met him at the dieting stage, I figured he wouldn't understand and I didn't even try to explain.

2. Most fat people weren't born fat

As far back as I can remember, I always loved food. I was crazy over food. Any kind of food.

I always loved whatever food that was served to the table—fried, steamed, cooked, fruits, vegetables, meat, chicken, fish, sweet, salty, everything was appealing and delicious.

I grew up in a family that appreciates good food. In my parents' home, my mother cooked every sort of food that could be imagined (except coffee and sushi). My late grandmothers, who were from the Holocaust survivors' generation, were constantly worried that my brother and I were not eating enough. In my brother's case, it may have been so; but in my case, not at all. I was always willing to taste, eat, add a little more to my plate and finish it all, to the last crumb.

They were always pleased with me for "cleaning up my plate."

"Always" was more or less until third grade.

In third grade, I met the doubtful pleasure known as dieting. That was in 1980. My mother "introduced me to the club." She was overweight and went on diets, and I was about to follow in her footsteps. I was plump, not fat, but rather big. I was an ideal candidate for joining the "diet movement."

I began using saccharine (in my coffee) in third grade. It took me 15 years to decide that I was finished with that poison, and another two years of withdrawal (I switched to two teaspoons of sugar, and gradually less…) until I got used to coffee without sugar.

From that point on, I went on diets. On my own, with my mother, with a group, with a friend…any partner combination you can imagine. There wasn't a diet that I didn't try. Perhaps a cabbage diet, but that went unnoticed.

I started out on each diet with lots of willpower and a "decision" that "from now on, this is it! I'm not touching carbohydrates, proteins, sweet food, salty food, baked food, fried food…", each diet and its special twist. I changed my menu from top to bottom overnight. I lost weight, I held on for a week/month/two months/ half a year (**depending on which method of torture was chosen**) and then I couldn't stand it anymore and gained it all back. With lots of extras.

I enlisted in the Israeli army as thin as could be (after a diet, of course). As I mentioned before - I gained 67 lbs during the two and a half years of army service, which I began a size 12 and ended a size 22.

After my army service, I went back to the diets. **I lost weight again, but sure enough—I gained it all back.**

I continued this endless cycle until that horrible day when small blood clots appeared all over my body. This was because of a severe lack of protein in my body that was a result of a diet I was on for a few months. In this diet I took some natural based pills that made me lose my appetite almost completely. The physical damage to my body, those scary blood clots, made it clear to me that **that was it, I was through with diets**.

3. The stories we live by

I grew up in a home where there was always plenty of food—warm, tasty and fresh. Great food. Food that you can't find in the best restaurants, because my mother is simply an expert cook.

She loves to cook and bake, she loves to try out new recipes from all ethnic origins, from all countries and of all kinds.

My mother is a master chef in cooking and baking. Whatever she prepares is delicious: kreplach and veronicas (Polish oriental food), perfect chicken soup, filo and pastry doughs, mousse cakes, tort cakes, fruit pies, ikra (Romanian fish egg dish) and chareime (moroccon oriental-style fish), beef stroganoff, Italian minestrone soup, French onion soup, home-made jam….and many more yummy dishes. I always enjoyed eating the dishes she prepared, they were all so delicious.

I always admired her patience and her efforts to appeal to the special taste of every family member. My mother will prepare for each member of the family the special dish that she likes: fried, salty, sweet, with oil, without oil, you name it.

For instance, I became a vegetarian when I was 17, and until my daughter was born when I was 32, I didn't touch meat. During all my vegetarian years, I got to eat whatever everyone else had, but in its vegetarian version because **my mother insisted I enjoy the flavors everyone else did**. It's crazy from my point of view; you really need to be into it to enjoy making such a huge effort to please everyone's taste.

Thing is, I always thought that I was exactly like her.

But over the last years, I've realized that I'm not my mother, and today I know that my attitude to food, cooking and the kitchen in general is very different from hers.

I don't have the patience to cook according to recipes, I won't touch yeast or fish, and you won't catch me preparing anything too complicated. I don't mean that I don't enjoy preparing food, and I think I'm quite a good cook actually, but I get that urge for cooking at certain times and with certain dishes.

My approach to the kitchen has gone through a dramatic change since the day I **allowed** myself to step back and check my real feelings toward it. It wasn't a simple task to do when I was the only one to handle the change, imagine what a child or a family member has to go through if her approach towards food is different from the others'?

The answer is quite clear: chances to change childhood habits are low, not impossible, but quite difficult as there are always the people around us who don't make it any easier to change. Apparently, the habit applied **to stop eating** sweets, pastries, fried foods or salty foods **is very similar to the habit to eat** them.

After weight loss surgery, these habits confront the operated and their supporting family & friends with **this huge challenge**. Everyone (the operated and her close community) must be able to **accept** that **the operation creates a new situation** in which the operated person is in a new process of learning what and how much she wants to eat. The ability to continue sitting together with everyone around the table is crucial for the success of this procedure.

This situation is a complicated one because on top of the pressure coming from everyone around you regarding what and how much you eat, you don't even know the answers… **A person who has just had a weight loss surgery doesn't know what and how she should eat or drink and what amount of food her stomach can handle.** The conflict with her old habits is challenging, and having everyone around give good advice can be overwhelming.

Another factor that concerns habits and makes adjustment harder are the **excuses**; excuses that we tell ourselves like, "I'm fat because my mother was always piling food on my plate," or "I'm fat because of my age," or "My parents are Holocaust survivors and at home we learned never to throw food away." After weight loss surgery, you get the priceless opportunity to re-examine everything you say or think about food…Is it really forbidden to throw out food? Are you going to go on eating everything served to you just because that's what you're used to? Does everyone around you really know what they're talking about when they give you advice regarding what you should be eating?

Try to avoid judgment and criticism. If you'll take a careful look at the habits of people around you and check well-known "truths," I think you'll be surprised to discover that they are the results of years of **education**, of cultivating the image of the "Polish mother," of PR, advertisements and media, all are part of our lives from day one and they have such a strong influence on how we think.

Weight loss surgery is not brain surgery. **After the operation, your brain will stay exactly the same**, as well as those of the people around you. The more you adapt a different way of thinking, the more you **examine conventional ideas** of approaching food and body image. **Check your limits** and investigate your surroundings **before** surgery; it will make it easier for you to accept the change that will come afterwards and you'll be able to develop a new lifestyle.

No one can tell you what, when and how much to eat. That was true before surgery, and it's even more so afterwards.

The operation is your opportunity to find out **how** to eat only when you are hungry, even if it means to eat nine times a day, and even if it doesn't please your family members who are used to eating promptly three times a day! It's also an opportunity to decide **what** you want to eat—your new stomach doesn't let you eat a lot, so choose what you want to eat very carefully. Is that what you really like? Is that what's best for your body? Is that what really tastes the best? Take a moment and think about these issues—have you ever let yourself ask these questions?

You can eat fried chicken all day if that's what you like, you can eat only bread if you want, and you can eat nuts, almonds, fruits and vegetables. **You can choose how to live your life** and what nutrition is best for your body. These are your decisions, and only yours, as well as the responsibility for the consequences.

It's not easy to say goodbye to sayings that we've grown up with, and some of them have become a part of us; sayings that we pass on to our children, like "clean your plate," "if you don't eat you won't grow/the policeman will come/you'll stay hungry."

In many cultures what makes a home warm and cozy is the amount and variation of the food served; but this is insane—you certainly don't love your children any less if they get to eat according to their hunger, eating pace and taste.

Take a look at your comfortable home and enjoy being a role model for your kids. What if at the holiday evening table, you served less food? Is it possible your guests might actually like it? I am sure it is. A happy home doesn't depend on the food served at the table! The success of a social event doesn't have to be measured by the food that is served; family gatherings that are all about the food served are all so common, can't we just enjoy the get-together itself?

Creating an "accepting" relationship with your food and your body is very important for recuperating from your operation and for success in this new chapter in your life. It's especially important during the period when, on one hand, you won't be able to live according to your old habits, but on the other hand, you'll have to learn how to cope with the results of the operation. No one, including family and friends who want your best, will be able to help you at this point. On the contrary, most likely that with their best intentions and knowing your former habits (and theirs), they'll get in the way. The **less** you get advice from others, the more you will be able to learn your new stomach and what **really** suits you, what you can take from your past habits, and how you want your new lifestyle to be.

4. Stop abusing your body

When I was 25, I was as thin as I ever was, after taking natural diet pills. To this day, I have no idea what ingredients they contained. The "magic pills" were guaranteed to suppress appetite and cause weight loss. And they did.

They were so great that I completely lost my appetite, and lived on an apple a day, sometimes eating a slice of cheese in addition to it. I lost 50 lbs in four months. I felt wonderful, I looked great and I went out and bought myself new clothes, including a designer dress from an exclusive boutique.

I woke up one morning and discovered blue blotches as big as 2-2.7 inches in diameter on my legs, hands, stomach…I had **frightening** spots all over my body. They looked like black-and-blue marks (in medical terms, hematoses), but it wasn't after an accident or a fight, and they didn't hurt. They were just there.

The doctor I went to immediately diagnosed **lack of protein**. Apparently, my body didn't get enough protein because I had lost my appetite due to the "wonder pills," and it began "eating away" the layer of protein that covers the veins and capillaries. As a result, these blood clots appeared. On doctor's orders, I was to immediately stop taking these "magic pills" and start a diet just as extreme—I **had to give my body plenty of protein** as quickly as possible. I ate the "whites" of six eggs for breakfast, the "whites" of six eggs for lunch, and the same for supper for the next 4-5 days, in addition to drinking plenty of water.

The blood clots disappeared within a week, and during the next few months, my healthy appetite returned, and I gained back more than 67 lbs…

I never gave away the designer dress that I had bought...it's still in my closet. It's almost the only souvenir I still have from that time in my life. Actually, I do have one more memory—the fear I felt when I saw those giant blue spots all over my body. **I think it was then that I first realized that poor nutrition could really harm you.**

As a result of that medical catastrophe, I decided to **stop dieting**. I stuck to that decision ever since, and I continued to put on more weight. Some said I was damaging my health, but I knew that going on yet another diet was not the solution for me.

Despite my obesity (at my peak, I weighed almost 287 lbs), and aside from what I saw in the mirror, I was happy. I refused to be unhappy simply because I was obese, "because obese people, as you know, can't really be happy."

My life was always full of satisfaction, curiosity, and self-fulfillment. I have wonderful children and an ex-husband who was like a friend. I am an entrepreneur, a designer, I create, volunteer and own a business that I established by myself. I consult and guide designers in marketing their work on etsy.com through my online

Marketing School at limitz.co.il (you're welcome to come in and join!), and I love my job. I always surrounded myself with friends that made me happy and my life was, and still is, full of creativity, color, and enjoyment.

There was one issue, though, that I couldn't find a solution for—how to eat right without going on a diet. One day I happened to stumble upon a website that made me feel I was about to solve the big mystery of my life. On that day, I first heard of a way of life called the "non-diet approach." I found a local mentor who taught this mental approach towards food, and this had an influence on my life from then on.

The important lessons that I learned regarding this new way of thinking helped me cope with life after the operation, and I'll go into more detail later in the book. At that stage, I felt that I was ready to face what lay ahead for me, even though I wasn't sure I really knew what that meant.

From my optimistic point of view, the "non-diet" approach that I began to learn and decided to embrace showed promising results! I realized that I could lose weight without suffering, without diets, without starving myself and without doing harm to my body. I realized that I had found a method of living that could lead to success. The pounds that started flying away were the bonus; the mental road I was on was the main thing.

While examining the process I lost 9 lbs without dieting. This was a sign for me that I had found something I could really use in an ongoing manner and apply to my life. I realized that I had found the key to a sane way of approaching food, but I felt that wasn't enough. I couldn't begin the long and tiring process of getting control on my way of living on my own. I began a process of mentally healthy eating habits. Back then, while I weighed almost 286 lbs, my eating patterns were changing. **No one noticed this change, it was subtle and almost minor to the external world (i.e. everyone), but I knew the change had begun.**

Two years later, I decided to have a weight loss surgery. There are a few bariatric operations around, and I chose the Gastric Sleeve surgery.

What is Gastric Sleeve surgery?

Sleeve surgery is an operation that reduces the size of the stomach, belonging to a group of several bariatric operations.

"Bariatric surgery (weight-loss surgery) includes a variety of procedures performed on people who are obese. Weight loss is achieved by reducing the size of the stomach with a gastric band or through the removal of a portion of the stomach (sleeve gastrectomy or biliopancreatic diversion with duodenal switch) or by resecting and re-routing the small intestine to a small stomach pouch (gastric bypass surgery(" (from Wikipedia, "Bariatric surgery").

A weight loss surgery is an operation by all parameters. It is performed under general anesthesia, and through small openings in the stomach, the surgeon inserts surgical instruments that inflate the abdomen, and with the help of an optic lens and scalpels, allowing him to proceed with surgery.

Is this a simple operation? I've heard people who went through this procedure that said that "the day after the operation, you will get up and go to work." For some people I got to know, that's the way things turned out. **My experience was different.** For two weeks after the operation, I had the most terrible nausea ever and couldn't stop vomiting. It took me more than a month to get myself together. Physically, after the surgery aside from the nausea and vomiting, I had no side effects. Fortunately, I suffered no pain at any stage and didn't need painkillers. **Everything seemed to be all right.**

The thing is that along with the physical effects of the operation, **something else happens to you.** At this point, you realize that you have done something very drastic and that from now on, you have to deal with the consequences.

Aside from reducing the size of the stomach, which causes weight loss, **the weight loss operation has an effect on the brain**. I am not referring to the release of substances of any kind…I am talking about your thoughts, your behavior, the effect on your everyday lifestyle and also the new attitude of people around you, which brings us back to the starting point—what happens within your head?

You can see the results of the operation almost immediately as there is a dramatic weight loss. Along with your new looks, you get an unexpected bonus. Actually, you get a whole pack of bonuses. In the next chapter, I will tell you about the big "bundle of benefits" you will receive after your operation.

Why did I decide to undergo weight loss surgery?

On a winter morning in early December 2012, while sitting in my car outside the neighborhood supermarket, the phone rang. My mother was on the line.

"I have something to tell you," she says, "I just saw a television program about health and nutrition, and there was an interview with a well-known professor who spoke about the sleeve operation your friend had a few months ago."

"O.K., did he say anything new?"

"He spoke about the operation itself, about the people who undergo it, about the astounding results...and listen, I think you should really think about it...you're over 40, you're still healthy, but we both know things are not going to get any better...the family tendency to diabetes is heading your way, we've seen the results of your tests. I think you should seriously consider having this operation. You have your whole life ahead of you, and you have two small children to think about. **Now is the time.**"

I didn't answer. It wasn't the first time my mom and I had discussed the subject. My mother and I have both struggled with our weight since forever. Years of going through diets together have shown us what diet is about, how difficult it is, the joy of losing weight and the despair of regaining it all back. I think that **we have gone through dozens of diets together**. I estimate that overall, we have lost and gained **thousands of pounds**. Not only that, two uncles and two cousins of mine have had weight loss surgery in the last decade. As you might realize by now, obesity is quite a common problem in our family.

I stopped going on diets when I became pregnant at the age of 31. I gave birth to my sweet Libi, and then, at the age of 33 I gave birth to another baby, my Matan. But I gained something else during this period—67 unexpected pounds.

I wouldn't go on a diet again. The reason I stopped going on diets in the first place was because I understood this was not the right way to lose weight. I think I was mature enough at that point in life to realize that going to extremes just doesn't work. Not in your job, not in relationships, certainly not when it comes to food or sports.

Going to the extreme means to walk on the **edge**, and it's relevant to any field in your life, including your patience and your ability to cope with your everything life brings. **You can't stay on the edge for very long.** This is what happens when you go on a diet. You can eat lettuce for weeks and even months and see the lbs fly away, but when it comes to the **test of persistence—** it just doesn't last, and you gain it all back.

So if going on a diet is not the solution, what is?

It is a very drastic move to choose the procedure of elective surgery to lose weight. Not only was I against it, I felt sorry for those who chose to go on with it and gave in to the surgeon's scalpel. I believed there was another way, and I was sure it had to do with the "non-diet" approach. I changed my own attitude towards food after a "non-diet approach" workshop where I learned and discovered a new way of managing my life and food; so I knew there **was** another way. There was nothing "instant" about it, but to get long-term results with your habits of eating—"instant" does not work.

While practicing the non-diet approach, I lost four pounds without a diet, only by agreeing to learn once again how to listen to myself. I had **agreed to examine** my food and eating habits. I learned about emotional eating, and I found myself examining my own statements and others deeply. **I realized that the approach to food I grew up with does not suit me or the life that I live.**

I realized that in order to maintain a healthy body, fat or thin, I **have to maintain a healthy brain**. I began by thoroughly examining every social axiom that I grew up on, and then I was ready to face the consequence of refusing to accept them.

I knew back then that my way to approach food issues **was not common** in society, that I was very likely to get disapproving and disagreeing faces back at me, and I could see why. **Up till then, I always went with the flow, I was part of it, and I agreed to those**

common beliefs! I agreed that…"We must eat six small meals a day, or three normal sized meals, that we should engage in sports at least three times a week, avoid carbohydrates/fat/proteins," and so on. I used to accept every new way to lose weight completely, but **I had decided that this was it.** I wasn't going along with statements of any kind anymore. I refused to accept any guidelines or limitations about what is right or wrong for you according to the latest fashion/health news or research. This was the first time I really accepted myself at the weight of 264.5 pounds.

If we go back to the conversation I had with my mother, I realized that **to go on with my new approach, I needed physical help**, and I agreed that a smaller stomach would offer me that help.

"I think you're right," I told my mom. "I'm going to have this operation. I'm going to find out what tests I have to do, and then I'll call my doctor."

We hung up, and I immediately initiated the process. I called a friend who had been through the operation for support and practical advice, then called my family doctor requesting him to prepare the test forms, and involved the health insurance company to find out what I was entitled to ("100% of the cost, just choose your doctor and hospital!").

My examination test results brought news with them—they showed that I had a fatty liver I didn't know about and gallstones (which I learned from my doctor were not necessarily connected to obesity). I consulted with a surgeon as well as a psychologist and a dietician and then the day of the operation was scheduled.

I made the decision on December 23, 2013. The operation was scheduled for February 19, 2014.

Within two weeks of the decision, with private insurance and a BMI that guaranteed me complete coverage, I had completed all the necessary tests. After two months of preparation, I underwent the weight loss operation as scheduled.

Nothing and nobody had prepared me for what was waiting for me from that day on.

Is this operation a must?

1. Preparation

Whether you're months or days before surgery, I think you should get prepared, and the sooner, the better. I believe you should know what you are expected to undergo, and you **can do this by** learning beforehand what can improve the life that awaits you in the new format (format = body + brain/soul). **You will be leaving the operating room with a new stomach, but your mind and habits will stay exactly the way you left them a few hours ago.** Beware of anyone telling you that as a result of the operation you will be thin and healthy. This focus is partly true because there is a lot more to it and setting these expectations is not accurate and is not giving you the whole picture.

You might prefer to prepare on your own or maybe join a support group and a mentor to lead you through the process (that's what I did, but note what the focus was on—eating habits and their part in our life!). Either way you chose is fine as long as you learn how to approach your eating habits in a new way.

I do encourage you to join a support group before the operation, in order to come as prepared as much as you can for the situation in which you have a new stomach and an old mind. I believe that knowledge is power, which is why I chose to share my experience with you.

2. Keeping your body in balance

To undergo the operation successfully, I suggest you concentrate on three goals:

1. Leave the operation room in a good state
2. Approach the operation in the healthiest state you can achieve
3. Listen to your gut feeling and go with your heart (don't let anyone know better than you anymore!)

You don't really have much control over the first goal. I hope that you have chosen the surgeon carefully and that your operation will be successful as most weight loss operations usually are.

Concerning the second goal, I will go into detail in this chapter, but allow me to share with you what I learned regarding a healthy body: a healthy mind derived from loving yourself as you are, moving around (a.k.a. sports) and good food that you really like.

As for the third goal, I will explain in detail since it concerns a variety of fields in our lives that go under change after the operation, and each one of them requires to be dealt in a different way.

My advice comes from my experience. I am not a psychologist, I haven't studied psychology, and I am not trying to give anyone psychological advice. My target is to share with you different situations that you or someone you know that went through a weight loss procedure have to deal with, so that if you face it you can recognize the situation and understand the complexity of becoming a skinny person in a very short time. A weight loss operation is a drastic measure, which brings with it drastic results in a short and…drastic time.

As I mentioned before, I'm against going to the extreme in any field in your life. In the case of weight loss surgery, it can't be avoided. **The body reacts to a**

small amount of food very quickly, and the weight loss begins immediately. This is enough drastic change for a lifetime, and I think you shouldn't adapt to more extreme changes during this period of your life.

I believe that if you aim for long term success—nothing should be done too drastically, and this surgery is for life; so from the pre-operation stage, and certainly afterward you should maintain a stable approach to changes. Sports are fine, but don't overdo; healthy food is fine, but don't overdo; the expectations built around the physical operation results are drastic ones. Your body IS going to go through a huge change, your brain isn't, which is why this build up bothers me. **The fewer changes you'll need to go on your habits after the operation the more likely it is to succeed for the long term.** Take a moment and look back—how long have your "forever" decisions—such as "from today I'll exercise every day, begin a diet, walk three kilometers a day or swim several laps in the pool three times a week"—last?

How long were you able to stick to them?

Sure, there are people who are able to stick with "forever" changes for years. Most of us don't.

I want to offer you a different and more relaxed approach to your habits and way of living.

Consider the operation **as an opportunity to change big things in baby steps.** Let's be real, there's no need to make things harder on yourself in addition to the enormous changes caused by the operation. If you adopt this approach, you'll increase your chances of sticking to every small decision you will make. Changes will appear slowly but surely, and you will benefit from them.

3. What habits can support the success of weight loss surgery?

a. The Non-Diet Approach

I found out about this approach by accident while surfing on the web way back in 2012. I Googled something like "losing weight without going on a diet" and landed right into a whole new world of information. The concept of losing weight without dieting fascinated me. Here was a sane and logical alternative to diets and surgery. I finally found a new approach to life!

I studied the method thoroughly and found it very appealing. I learned that I might be able to lose weight by changing my way of thinking, and I am not referring to hypnosis or magic….

This way of thinking offered a completely different approach to food, different from all the diets that I had undergone since third grade. Here was an approach of forgiveness and compassion, a way of examining what I ate with open eyes, and most importantly, a way to accept the way I look.

So I tried it, and it worked! I felt good without starving myself, without suffering. I felt I won a battle without fighting. It was clear to me that this was the key to healthy eating, the solution I had been searching for years.

I always knew there **must be another way**, but I had no idea what it was. I felt I had found it!

I joined a group of people, some fat, some thin, some with average weight, older and younger…for the first time I met people coping with bulimia, anorexia and "just" other obese people like me who were anxious all their lives to lose weight but didn't…here I met all the varied results of our eating diseases in our sick society.

Deep into this workshop I joined, I heard about **emotional eating for the first time in my life**; for the first time I was taught to feel hunger; for the first time I was taught to identify the feeling of a full stomach.

I learned to listen to my body; I learned that **I don't really like everything I eat**; I learned to realize that I was eating food that I didn't really want to eat, and **I learned to stop** eating food that doesn't really appeal to me. I actually learned to refuse food, and I even learned that food can be thrown into the garbage! I learned how to put down my knife and fork way before I finished eating the food on my plate, and I learned that not everything I was taught about food and eating was necessarily good for me.

I understood that even at the age of 38, you can and should learn new things about yourself, any age is great for having doubts for all the "musts" and "must nots" you were raised on, even if they were passed on with good intentions.

To my surprise, I found that I was losing weight without eating lettuce and lean cheese…a miracle had happened! I enjoyed the food I tasted, I wasn't dieting, and I was losing weight!

The group was very supportive and stimulating on a daily basis, I got to know friends who shared a common problem, and I learned that "food illness" is shared by fat and thin people alike. For the first time, I met thin people with serious eating problems.

I was shocked to get to meet people whose sense of happiness depended on whether they ate a square of chocolate or not. I realized that I was quite different from others as far as my opinions about food and my body. Not that I was overjoyed about being overweight, but I wasn't depressed about it, and it didn't manage my life.

After months of study and practice, I left the group weighing 9 lbs pounds less and feeling that I had found the key. Despite that, I gained the weight back with extras in a few months. At this point, at the peak of my weight, I weighed 282 lbs, but I knew there was no turning back, and **what I had learned about myself**

in these months was here to stay. It was so clear and logical, and I had seen it work. I had changed my feelings towards food, and I was not going to give in. Now was the time to practice, because only practice makes perfect.

Actually, when I came to think of it, I've done this before. I recalled that in my twenties I wanted to stop drinking saccharine in my coffee. It took me two years to go from saccharine to coffee without sugar. That is exactly what showed me the way now. **I decided to** focus on **practice**, and I knew that gradually the **process would become a part** of my everyday life.

I made small changes in various fields in my life. After years of wearing nothing but black clothes, I began to buy clothes in other colors, in my size, and I kept examining my feelings, testing how people around me reacted, and it taught me a lot.

I learned that people around me judged me focusing mainly on how I looked. Fortunately, I am a friendly and open person, my friends are very warm and encouraging, and I enjoyed each and every comment.

I noticed that even when I didn't lose weight, but I smiled, for instance, people would say, "Oh, you lost weight!" or "You look great!"

Like most of us, I also want to be pretty and attractive, and this new approach to my looks fascinated me.

As I had predicted, my new approach to food wasn't accepted very well by my family and friends. At that point, I needed all the strength and resources I had gotten from the "non-diet" support group, so I focused on the latter to stay strong with my new way.

b. Small baby steps

Common knowledge is that we are born with a mechanism of hunger and satiation according to our body's needs. Considering the **brainwash** we go through in childhood, it's a wonder that some of us still have this mechanism as adults. For most of us, this mechanism is disrupted as the years go by due to education, social pressure, trends, and fashion.

Come to think of it, who said we must eat 3 meals a day? Who said we must eat 6-7 small meals throughout the day? Aren't we expected to eat only when we are hungry?

Why do we listen to someone else instead of listening to our body? As babies and infants, we are dependent on others for our food. Does this mean we have to eat when they think we are hungry? How many parents manage to understand when their baby is really hungry and that her crying is because of food or thirst and not for other reasons? So, what age is it ok for someone else to decide what's good for you to eat?

I feel the answer is obvious. It's your body and in no way someone else is able to decide how, when, how much and what you should eat; but, for cultural habits and reasons as stated above, this mechanism is interrupted from the day we are born.

As part of the complete change in my approach to food, **I stopped listening** to what others said about "the right way to eat." I accepted the fact that no one knows better than me how and what I should eat, but I had one problem…If I wanted to eat according to my body's needs, I had two alternatives: either to be reborn or to learn from scratch. I can't be reborn so learning, like a baby beginning to take his first steps, was the chosen alternative and I decided I was going to make it possible slowly but surely. These were my baby steps.

It was achievable because I relied on the first signs of success that I had experienced when I applied the non-diet approach, signs that reminded me that if I had lost weight without dieting…everything was possible.

When I understood that these mechanisms can be relearned and that I have the key to it, I felt a sense of strength. I was still very fat, but relaxed on the food "front." I had stopped struggling, not because I had given in, but because I had made a clear decision and had a definite direction to go in.

I went through several incidents in my life at the time—I got divorced, moved to a new house and established a new business, but as far as my relation with food, I took things calmly. I practiced this new approach to food for a couple of years, and then one day I decided to go through the weight loss surgery. How can that be? you might ask. The answer is that what I learned about myself and practiced two years before the operation **helped me cope with the after-**

surgery state of mind and practically kept me sane. I mean to say that I knew how to eat with a tiny stomach, and there were minimal tense incidents around this issue. My thought is that if I learned and taught myself from scratch by daily practice, you can too.

c. What did this practice involve?

I practiced listening to my body when I eat, but not in a spiritual way—I really wanted to see how it felt to be full, and it was complicated. To feel full having a stomach of a fat person is not easy. I never knew how it felt to be full when I was obese. I didn't even know what I was looking for. Only after the operation, I understood.

I was very aware of what I ate, and I tried to eat mainly food that I liked very much, even if they were **considered fattening**, like nuts and fried chicken. I decided that if I ate lots of food, it should at least be food that I like the most; I decided to respect the food that I liked.

I chose to exercise my body in the only way I really enjoyed—riding a bike. I called it leisure time in motion, and later on, it was a rescue for my skin when

I became thin. Before the operation, I apparently didn't look too great on a bicycle, because I remember hearing remarks from a group of children who watched me ride with my children. One of them said, "Wow, did you see that giant woman riding a bike?"

I just didn't care. I enjoyed it so much, and **I decided to concentrate on the pleasure** it gave me. I stopped thinking about what everyone else thought, young and old, and I really didn't understand—if I enjoy riding my bike, why should I care about what others think about it?

Like I said the decision to listen only to myself brought a lot of disapproval from my family and friends. To be able to cope with it, I had to accept certain feelings within me and decide to believe that I knew what was right for me. For example, I had to accept the fact that although I had been sure all my life that I loved chocolate, that wasn't really so. I mean I do like chocolate, but only chocolate of the best quality. I really don't care for ordinary milk chocolate, and I have to taste other kinds of chocolate before I know I like them.

I explored what hunger feels like. I didn't starve myself, but I stopped automatically eating three meals a day. I stretched the meal times and examined what I felt when lunchtime passed, for example. I had to do this because I hadn't experienced any days of hunger in my life, so how was I expected to know what it feels like without experimenting?

Last but not least, I was concentrating on feeling happy and accepting myself as I was, despite my weight.

The reaction of people around me was the opposite. Words were not said, but eyebrows were lifted when I didn't finish everything on the plate. The scolding and sometimes insulted looks were enough. But I chose to ignore them; I chose the way I felt was right for me.

During this period I got divorced, gained knowledge in my area of expertise—digital marketing from the best teachers in the world, established a business in which I show designers the way for international online sales, traveled with the children throughout the country and the world, bought a bicycle I had dreamed of for years and enjoyed life.

All this happened during the two years before I went through the weight loss operation, **before I had any idea I would have surgery.**

In those two years, I changed my attitude toward food. I changed my attitude to more areas in my life, but I hadn't raised it back then. I just knew I was satisfied with my life and definitely happy, and I had no idea what this would lead to.

Sweet secrets in the cupboard

One of the remarkable applications of the non-diet approach in my everyday routine was the twist it had on my attitude towards the candies I had around the house.

When I was a little girl, my mother used to hide candies around the house. This was not some kind of game, she wanted to control the amount of candy and chocolate my brother and I ate. She also wanted to have control of the time we consumed it. We didn't have a candy cupboard or a candy drawer within our reach. The snacks were hidden in many places around the house, in the bedroom closet, above the winter blankets, behind cans and jars in the kitchen closets and more.

My brother and I developed a game. When my parents would leave the house, we went on a candy hunt. My brother was always happy when my parents left us on our own because he knew that I wouldn't give up until I'd find some candy.

And I always did.

When I look back, I now realize that I was brought up to think that **candies are something you hide** from children, that you mustn't eat as much as you want of them, that candies come at certain times and in certain amounts, for example as a treat after a meal, that candies are never eaten before sleep or in the morning or just for no special reason.

This was something I took for granted and never gave a second thought until I was 38 years old.

Naturally, I raised my children in the same way: we had a "candy closet" way up high, they couldn't reach it, and I was responsible for the daily distribution.

The first thing I did when I tried to change my attitude toward food was to take the candies out from the top closet and put them in a special drawer **conveniently low and in the children's reach**, and please don't be mistaken—my kids like sweet stuff like everybody else!

My family thought that my decision was crazy, but I believed I was doing the right thing. Deciding was easy, carrying it out was challenging because I had taken a step that was unusual for me. I took a deep breath and **curiously waited to see what would happen**.

I went through two very difficult months, two months during which my children could walk over 24/7 to the candy drawer and take candies as much as they wanted to, and I did nothing to prevent it. I didn't say a word, I was very uneasy, I wondered if I hadn't gone mad, but I looked the other way as if nothing had happened. A week went by and the children were in the candy drawer at every opportunity they had; two weeks went by and things were the same, and I was gritting my teeth. And then, after three weeks, a very strange thing happened: my daughter lost interest in the candy drawer! I was shocked. I suddenly noticed that she would go to the drawer once in three or four days, take a candy and that was all…

My son went on for another two weeks, and then he calmed down as well! I looked at both of them, and **I couldn't believe it.** It worked!

They lost interest.

The minute I showed that I didn't care and didn't set limitations, food stopped being an attraction, it became a **non-issue.** When I say that it didn't attract them, I mean that the minute I removed limitations and showed them that the candies would always be there, the children understood that there was no pressure, that they could come and take a candy whenever they felt like it, and they didn't have to devour lots of candies at once because "they might be gone."

A few years have gone by since then, and I am still curiously on the watch. I watch them from the living room and see that there are days when they don't get near the drawer at all; there are days when they snack a bit more; there are moments (of boredom, for example) when the candy drawer attracts them especially; there are meals with a treat and meals without one. I have realized that my children have more interesting things to do than going to the candy drawer, and I understand I prove to be right—**nobody on earth has the right or knowledge to tell anyone else when she is hungry or full or when she feels like having some sweets.**

"My bicycle and I"

When my brother and I were children, we were not allowed to ride our bicycles on Yom Kippur out of respect for tradition.

I remember how disappointed I felt every Yom Kippur when all my friends rode their bikes around the neighborhood, and I had to wander around with another girlfriend and see everyone having fun and feel jealous…

I promised myself that when the time came, I would allow my children to ride their bikes on Yom Kippur. From the moment they could ride by themselves, their father and I (mostly their father) ran after them.

We spent Yom Kippur of 2010 without their father because we had already divorced. I knew that I couldn't run after two small children who rode their bikes all over the place. Luckily, my sister-in-law and my brother were abroad and had left me my sister-in-law's bike.

This is how I found myself at the age of 39, for the first time in my life, riding a bike on Yom Kippur, not to mention that I hadn't been on a bicycle since I was 13 years old.

I rode the bike, and I can't describe how thrilled I was! It was so much fun, exactly like my childhood memories when I would ride with my brother and father. Those were the days when riding on the side of the main road between Rishon Lezion and Nes Tziona (my home town and the closest city), wasn't dangerous at all (back then it was a small side road and now it's a highway road, can you imagine that?)

Back to Yom Kipur: I got on the bike feeling a bit uncertain at first. After all, for more than 20 years I hadn't done this, but then…I felt such a sense of freedom, what a wonderful feeling!

My children, four-year-old Matan and six-year-old Libi, both looked at me with a mixture of shock and joy. I guess they couldn't have imagined me on a bike until then, even though I had promised them we would go riding on Yom Kippur!

We rode out the gate of town onto the main road, and as we peddled, a father went by with his son, and the boy said, "Wow Dad, look at that fat woman on a bicycle!"

I hadn't given it a thought until that moment. I probably looked like an elephant on wheels…certainly an unusual sight:-)

It was really strange, especially because I felt as light as a feather.

I didn't care at all what they said or thought, and even now it amuses me, because I felt so wonderful, and I still feel that way when I get on my bike.

In less than a month, I bought myself a bicycle. I decided that even though I wasn't in the greatest financial situation after the divorce, I would buy myself a new and top quality bicycle.

With help from my parents and my brother, who knows a lot about bicycles, I added a few nice accessories, got an upgraded bicycle seat, and even a pole that connected my son's bicycle to mine so that we could ride throughout the country.

That winter we moved to a new apartment, and I rode my bicycle around the new neighborhood. I also went on an enjoyable ride with my father and brother along the beach of Rishon Lezion and discovered a lake that had a bike road around it, about 4.5 miles of biking through fields in full spring blossom was pure pleasure.

One day I told a friend, who was also overweight, about my bicycle riding. I mean, I asked her if she owned a bike. It wasn't obvious that everyone owned one because I hadn't had one for more than twenty years…

"Sure, I have one, but I hate exercise," she answered.

I was taken by surprise with this answer: **Exercise? It's a bike, not a gym!**

When you enjoy doing something, even if someone calls it "exercise" (I also hate exercise, but what does that have to do with it?), it doesn't matter at all. It's simply so much fun!

There are people that **would love to dance but don't dare to do so because they're fat**, so they give it up because they're embarrassed about the way they look…

There are people who would love to stroll in the park and take walks in the fresh air, but they don't dare because they are fat. They dread the attention they might receive because of how they look, so they miss out the fun, relaxation and fresh air.

I don't get it. If that's what you like, who cares what you look like? How easy is it to surrender to choose to stay in the comfort zone, when at the same time you could really do something that makes you feel good?

Do you think it was easy for me to ride 4.5 miles with four uphill intervals? The last two of them almost knocked me out completely…it wasn't easy, I got off the bike and walked some of the way uphill. So what? These were two uphill intervals out of two and a half hours of a fantastic ride, good air and good company as well.

Is there something you're really passionate about doing but you give it up because you feel uncomfortable doing it? Please go out there and do it, from my experience I can tell you that it's a

pleasure. Exactly like it is to choose to eat only what you really like.

The story above is quoted from a blog post I wrote two years before the weight loss operation and I chose to add it to this book because it demonstrates the spirit of my approach to life at that time. I wasn't aware back then how important this approach was. I believed then, and even more so today, that **the most important thing in the world is my wellbeing**. Not in the antisocial sense. I would never do anything intentional that would hurt somebody. But if I enjoy doing something, I certainly won't give it up. It brings out the best in me. I feel great, and the people around me benefit from it too. It's a win-win situation.

The fact that I was able to enjoy the things that made me feel good, even though it seemed strange to others because of the way it looked, or because it seemed illogical or wrong in their opinion, was not only good for me mentally, but proved to be very helpful for my body after the operation. About six months after the operation, I noticed flabby skin under my arms, and frankly, it didn't look very good. I looked in the mirror and didn't like what I saw, but I reminded myself to take things in the right proportion and flabby skin under my arms was not the worst thing on earth.

By coincidence, a few days later, I joined a mountain bike riding group that met once a week in the Ben Shemen Forest, a 20 minutes' drive by car from my house. It was autumn in Israel, September 2013, and I was the first one to join the nature riding group that was led by Amos. He regarded it as exercise in nature (as well). I saw it as two hours of pleasure in the outdoors of nature with a growing group of new friends who happened to be on bikes like me.

The winter ended, spring arrived, and I was in front of the mirror again wearing a short-sleeved shirt. I couldn't believe my eyes. I had lost another 44 lbs since last summer, meaning that my arms were supposed to have looked even worse now, and it just didn't happen! Not only did they not look worse, but the flabby skin under my arms had shrunk!

Was that because of my weekly bike riding? Was it genetics? Had my body managed to adjust to the drastic change in my body's dimensions? I have no idea, and I really didn't have anything to compare to. At the age of 42 I didn't expect my body to be as firm as the body of a sixteen-year-old girl, so I guess it's a mixture of genetics, age and the exercise I did (and still do occasionally) as part of my leisure activity.

Self-acceptance is what really counts, and being able to discover the things that make you happy is the beginning of self-acceptance. If you enjoy swimming in a pool, go swimming! If you enjoy taking a walk in the park/forest/open air, go right ahead! If you like bicycle riding, find a riding group or buy a bike and go—what are you waiting for?

The more aspects of life you chose to fulfill, the more you get to live your life the way you really want to. But do this in baby steps, each time a bit more, and you will reach the point where you won't be thinking about food or other obsessions. I emphasize that I'm not referring to drastic steps. No complete change where you say, "From this day and on..." Looking for the things that make you feel good and choosing them is part of the change, whether it's choosing your friends or exercise or activities, including eating.

The more you add pleasurable activities to your life before the operation, including enjoyable exercise, the easier it will be for you to continue those activities afterward. **Ask yourself—do I really enjoy this activity?** If you don't enjoy it, go and find something else. You don't "have" to exercise, you should be enjoyably active; you don't "have" to eat lettuce, you should eat your favorite food; you don't "have" to avoid going to the beach or the pool in a bathing suit because you're fat, just go to the beach as much as you like if you enjoy it, don't think twice; and if you feel like taking a walk in the park or riding a bicycle, then go ahead and do it! Don't give up your happiness because of what people think or say, even if you actually look enormous in a sports outfit. Why do you need anyone's approval? You don't need anyone's approval for what you eat, how you eat, and when or what to wear in daylight, at night, on the beach or in bed. It doesn't matter how old you are, what your skin tone is or how much you weigh! You are free to choose what you wear and when, whether you are out getting fresh air, going for walks in the park, riding a bicycle or playing tennis…

The time for approval is over.

Practicing the life "after" the operation "before" you go through it

I learned the principles and exercised the "Non-diet approach" method for a few months and have been applying them years after, until they became part of my daily life. The new habits I've gained since have changed my approach to everyday activities, habits and and people around me, and not only towards food, so I would like to give you a sample of these exercises, whether you go through the operation or not. I think it's important to share with you, so that you can see what I practiced for quite a while. I suggest you try it. For each exercise, examine how you feel as it happens, see how people react, and see how you feel about it too.

1. **Refuse to eat!** Learn to say "no" when you are offered food that you don't like or an extra portion

when you are not hungry. Then, try this even if you really feel like having them.

2. Prepare a plate of food, sit down to the table, and in the middle of your meal, for no reason **get up and throw** the food into the garbage can.

3. Eat two tablespoons of food and **don't** take another one. Stay at the table with everyone until the end of the meal.

4. **Stop eating and drinking at the same time during your meal.** If you are used to eating and drinking at the same time, try to eat only, and then drink fifteen minutes later. You can do the opposite— drink a few sips and then wait fifteen minutes before you eat.

5. During a few days, every hour and a half or two, **eat whatever you want as much as you wish**. Write down the hours so that you will be sure to eat 7-8 times a day.

6. Combine exercises 4 and 5.

7. Eat only what **you really like**. Before you put a piece of food in your mouth, pause and ask yourself: Is this the food that I really want to eat now? If the answer is yes, enjoy eating it with no guilt feelings, and if it's not, leave it there or throw it away.

It's very important to practice these exercises when you are alone as well as when you are with family and friends. The purpose is to *simulate a real situation* that bariatric operated people experience and to examine three things:

1. How do you feel about the exercise?
2. What is your reaction *during* the exercise (Do you feel like stopping? Is it difficult? Does it sound crazy? Does it sound logical? Does it make you uncomfortable?)
3. Practicing the social situation that develops during the exercise—are others' reactions bothering you? Are they acting strange? Why are they pushing their nose? How are you coping with this interference? Do you remember it's your body and your decision what to do in this situation?

Practice each exercise for at least a couple of days. Decide in advance that you're devoting your time and will power, **even if it's not convenient, and especially if it's not**. The frustration and discomfort that you'll feel in each of these exercises should you decide to go through with the operation **will become very real for you after the operation**. Then these exercises will be "for real" a part of your life. This is not only weight loss, this is a new physical and mental lifestyle that will be part of your life from the day after your operation.

Here are a few more guidelines that I recommend:

1. Learn to **eat in a cheerful mood**, with no guilt feelings, without compromising! Take away thoughts like "just one more bite," or "this is going to stay in my fat body now forever."
2. Eat when you are hungry, **not when you are supposed to eat**.
3. **Eat what you really like**, not everything that is served.
4. **Learn to choose how, when and what to eat**. True, your eating habits are influenced by education and environment, but **after the operation this becomes meaningless**. This is your opportunity to learn new eating habits as an independent person who doesn't have to accept the advice of others.
5. **Your body is your most important asset**, and only you are really familiar with it. **Take charge and responsibility and don't expect anyone else to know better!**

If you decide to have surgery, **you will have to learn to get to know your body all over again**. Take advantage of this opportunity and prepare by practice. Enjoy the process, examine your attitude and that of the people around you, and take responsibility for your decisions. The strange part of it is that listening to yourself is actually a good way to approach food whether you feel fat or skinny! I met people who changed their lives with these exercises **and had no need for surgery**. This way of eating habits and approach toward food is recommended whether you intend to operate or not.

Life after surgery

The best advice I can give you before the operation is, as I mentioned before, **to live the day *after* the operation long *before* it comes.**

One of the important points I want to make is that **the operation doesn't change who you are**. Assuming that the operation will be successful, the main thing that happens is that you can't eat more than a very small amount of food at one time, and I mean a very small amount. A tiny amount.

On the other hand, your habits remain the same. In addition, you still have a sense of smell, and your appetite stays healthy!

So what and how do you choose to eat, when on one hand, the dissonance between wanting to eat and not being able to, can be unbearable but on the other hand, you want a healthy body, and food and health go together. So if you can only eat a small portion, **wouldn't you want it to be as delicious as possible?**

When you look at your life before the operation, do these two facts apply to you today?

You may likely say "no" **but that's what will happen right after surgery**, and if you aren't ready to face the answers before your operation, what would you do about it when there is no turning back?

I regret to tell you that nothing will change. You'll need a great deal of mental power to cope with these changes and others that I mention in this book. That's why I feel I was very lucky that during the two years before my operation, my attitude towards food was very much like that of the post-surgery period.

The main difference I saw between life before the operation and life afterward is the size of the stomach was the amount of food I could eat.

Since my operation, I can feel very clearly when I am hungry and when I am full. I can either try to "stretch" my stomach just a bit more, or put my knife and fork down and stop eating. But this was not a common thing for me, and it takes practice!

When I left the operating room, I was already prepared for a different way of eating, thanks to the practical tools I learned beforehand that enabled me to face the drastic change of the size of my stomach. My attitude towards food was very different from the attitude of most of my friends, both fat and skinny. The operation didn't change my habits, although some think they have.

In my opinion, **the success of a weight loss operation (or any bariatric operation for that matter) depends on changing your way of thinking** long before you reach the operating room.

The reason I suggest people should change their eating habits long before the operation is that **it takes time to change your habits**. We all know that, but when you've just had a weight loss operation, you seem to be the same, and you're trying to continue your familiar routine, and that is **impossible**.

To be better prepared for surgery, **I suggest you aim beforehand to minimize the adjustment period after the operation and thus prevent unnecessary turnovers.**

A while after the procedure I had minor stomach scars, nausea and no pain (I experienced no pain after it, not even for a minute), everything looked the same. But these were external marks as you go through a complete change as far as being able to eat! The change was **inconceivable!**

The operation is a physical matter but our approach to food is not. For decades now, with ads and brainwashing, it is influenced by the brain.

In our society, people have clear opinions about food and eating. Everyone has an opinion about what one should eat, how much and when. **Everyone knows what's best for us**. We've learned from our parents how meals are conducted, we've gotten used to eating at certain hours even if we're not hungry (this is known as "social eating"), on television we're shown young and/or post-surgery models as the ideal of beauty and advertisements for diets and diet products. Overweight people are immediately categorized as unhealthy and not good looking.

All this had, of course, a very strong influence on the way people related to me after the operation and the major weight loss.

I am not a psychologist, I didn't have the tools to understand what went through people's minds, so all I could do was observe. It felt as if I had stepped out of my body, trying very hard not to judge, trying to understand what it meant when people said, "You're thin."

Oddly enough, as I lost weight, I began to realize that I didn't want to "be thin."

I didn't want to be thin. I wanted to feel good about myself, I want to love myself and be healthy and self-fulfilled. I knew that thinness doesn't necessarily guarantee happiness. Sometimes it can cheer you up, but it certainly is not the main thing that makes me happy.

Luckily, as I have mentioned, I didn't suffer from major side effects, and the main change was the limited amount of food that I could eat in each meal, which I still appreciate very much. The operation helped me concentrate on eating the food I really like, instead of constantly eating whatever I saw near me.

I was told by many people that I had changed since the operation. That didn't seem right to me because, in my opinion, I didn't. I'm the same Limor as before, just ten sizes smaller.

Does a weight loss of 110+ pounds change a person?

My answer is—no! But there are changes, so what are they? Well, it took me months to figure that out. When you lose so much weight in such a short time, several things happen:

- **The weight loss is immediate and thus makes a shocking visual difference**—weight loss operations cause a weight loss of dozens of lbs in a short time. The change can be seen on a weekly and monthly basis, and it can't be ignored.
- **We don't understand what's happening**—this situation is **new** to us, and if we haven't prepared ourselves, we will be caught by surprise, and **surprises aren't always pleasant.**
- **People around us, in general, don't understand what's happening to us.** They don't know how to react.

So the change is a result of three factors combined—the physical change, people's reaction and yours, and they result in placing you in *a completely new situation!*

You haven't gotten used to your new body and haven't been able to decide if it's good or not—Do you like it? Is it annoying? Is it is disappointing? Is the weight loss going too fast? Too Slow? Everything is happening so fast, and people around you are already reacting, judging and criticizing, as usual.

For the first time in my life, I discovered that sometimes support and encouragement can make you feel **uneasy**. I was caught unprepared, and I am telling you, there were occasions where I found myself in an almost impossible situation where I didn't or practically had no idea how I was expected to react.

1. The psychologist at your service!

About two months after my operation, I weighed 45 pounds less than before. I was recovering, still weak, trying to get back to my routine, trying to understand what was happening to my body and my mind, looking at my new self in the mirror and realizing that people were constantly staring at me.

That morning, I had taken the children to school and was just about to take a walk around the neighborhood.

And then she got a hold of me, a thin woman with a figure some people would die for.

"I dreamed about you last night, can you imagine?" she says.

"???" I didn't answer.

"Yes, I dreamed that I gained 45 pounds in order to have the operation you went through and then lost those 45 pounds, just like you. It must be such a great feeling!"

I just looked at her and said nothing.

I didn't know what to say…so many thoughts crossed my mind at that moment: the complicated recovery from general anesthesia, the two weeks of horrible nausea, the feeling of weakness, the hair loss I was experiencing, the vitamins I was taking, the food that became so necessary for survival, the hours I found myself sleeping and the fatigue, not recognizing myself in mirror…while everyone around me, down to the last one, was taking part in building my new identity.

I felt very confused, and I didn't have a moment of rest. During the first six months after the operation, I was very tired. Nothing hurt, I was just exhausted. I guess it was a combination of keeping up a regular routine and the small amounts of food I managed to swallow.

I certainly couldn't describe the way I felt as "fun" or something to envy.

Before the operation, I didn't think things would be like this. When I had dared to think about "the day after," I mainly wondered what I would look like. I worried about the general anesthesia I was about to have for the first time in my life. I wanted it to be behind me, and I wondered what I would look like.

My appearance. That's what I had on my mind before surgery.

Even though I decided on the operation for health reasons, my health was reasonable in general, and the test results were good. It was only natural I would be curious about how I would look after it. I spent time thinking about "what will I look like?" It was the most tangible thing I could imagine. I wondered how the stomach looks after pregnancy, after the fat melts away…I wondered how I would look with wrinkles (my facial skin was firm from extra fat at an age when wrinkles normally appear). I wondered how much "flab" I would have under my arms, it runs in our family.

Now I realize that when I thought about the results of the operation, my mistake was in my focus. I focused on the trivial, not on the main thing. I knew I would be thin. I hoped everything would go smoothly and that I would be healthy. But I didn't think about **what I would go through** from the moment I left the operating room and for the rest of my life. When I was pregnant, just the same, I only wanted to be after the birth, I didn't think about what happens after that.

When I was pregnant, I had a friend who was expecting near my due date. She said that she wasn't worried about the delivery, she was thinking about life afterward with the new baby—the lack of sleep, the new responsibility, the change in family relations, the lasting changes.

We both had normal deliveries, but I was shocked by the change in my life afterward. My friend took things differently, in a calmer way. It's not that her life didn't change completely, she was simply more prepared, I wasn't.

If we compare that to the adjustment after the weight loss operation, I should have realized. I focused on the wrong thing: I worried for the Anastasia and wondered how I would look and didn't realize that there was something else involved.

I almost made the same mistake again.

Almost…

Because luckily, without knowing at all, I reached the dramatic change after the operation more prepared than when I gave birth. **A dramatic change that is very apparent from the outside, but within, in the mind, in the soul, has many significant consequences.**

2. How sick can society be?

Worshipping beauty and thinness **is an illness in itself.**

After weight loss surgery, most of the weight loss occurs in the first year. You lose dozens of pounds within 12 months. Some lose 30 lbs, some lose 60 lbs and some lose more.

I lost 45 lbs in the first two months.

A few weeks after the surgery, when I went back to my daily schedule—work, children, and home—I was surrounded by many caring people. I am fortunate to have wonderful friends and acquaintances. I'm very lucky, and that's why I am very careful about what I am about to say, because I don't want to offend anyone.

Throughout history, we have been told how a beautiful body should look. For example, in the Renaissance, a full, plump body was considered beautiful as we can see in the paintings and the statues of that period. We saw the complete change in the 1960s when Twiggy became the model of beauty, and extremely thin models were idolized.

I grew up on Barbie and Cinderella (that's a subject for another book), on the models of the 1980s that became thinner and thinner as time went by. We all went through this brainwashing to a certain degree, and we all heard of weight watching and this "thin" ideal of beauty.

For as long as I can remember, I wanted to be thin, but because I was so far away from the ideal, I realized in my early thirties that these diets wouldn't help me, and I just gave up.

If someone thinner than me stood by my side and complained that she had eaten an ice cream and now she wouldn't be able to eat for a week, I ignored her, but not on purpose. I simply thought to myself (or said to her, depending on our friendship), "you deserve it, you're thin."

After the operation, I was very busy with food, but I was mainly busy eating things that were good for my body. I ate so little that every time I could—I ate.

So, when I did eat, I was able to eat a very small amount of food, something like a half of a small container of yogurt. After a few months, I could have a whole container of yogurt. Today I can eat 100 grams of hamburger or two containers of yogurt. That's where I am; it's not the same for everyone, but more or less. The moment I feel full, I stop eating, and if I forget or try to have a little more, it literally hurts.

What really surprised me (and still does) were the reactions to my new looks. I would probably do the same if I were in their place. What shocked me was the fact that a lot of their remarks focused on me, but I didn't understand how they were related to me, to the fat girl inside of me.

For instance, some people would say: "You eat so little, how can you live on that?", "You **lost weight**, I can't seem to lose the 5-10 lbs that I have on my thighs…" and so forth.

I can't relate to statements like these. I think they're irrelevant. It's not even a matter of right or wrong. **Five, eight or ten lbs don't make a difference, and personally, I think that a woman with a full and healthy body looks great, especially when she smiles.**

The truth is that I always have the answers and know what to say, but being approached with these remarks, I was left speechless.

I lost 5-10 lbs **a week**; I ate very little (and that's how I eat to this day) because if I eat one more bite, I'll throw up. I just can't eat more than that. That's why I had the operation. I needed a physical reminder that I'm full or hungry.

I was a happy person when I was overweight. A lot of things could make me unhappy or bothered me but not being fat. I didn't long to lose 5 lbs. I didn't bother about the length of my dresses because I didn't feel like wearing them anyway. I always had boyfriends who proved to me that what attracted them was not the size of my clothes.

What would I have changed if I could in the process of the weight loss after the operation? I guess **that if I had lost weight more slowly, I would have had more time to adjust**. No wonder a pregnancy takes nine months. Nature took care of the adaptation of the changes the pregnant woman goes through, but loosing weight as a result of the surgeon's knife, doesn't give you that privilege, and you have to adjust, in a very short time, to many new and drastic changes **completely different than before.**

I decided to have surgery because I realized that without drastic intervention, I wouldn't be able to live the kind of life I that I wanted. Having your body shrink is a wonderful bonus, but it's **only a bonus.**

And because I really think so, I was stunned by the reactions I got.

My thoughts and as a result—this book is about the yearning for a healthy body, for a body fuller than the skinny body I had at the peak of my weight loss, and about the fact that most of my friends didn't realize that "a healthy mind in a healthy body" is not just a saying.

3. Physical side effects

In addition to the drastic weight loss, there are other things that your body undergoes. Everyone reacts differently, according to genetics, age, skin elasticity, etc. Some of the changes may be drastic, and if they come together with social pressure, it can be very challenging.

Some friends of mine who had the operation experienced some of these side effects, some didn't, and I experience some of them to this day.

Loss of appetite, a feeling of fullness and nausea – After the operation, the stomach is very small. How small? More or less the size of a banana. Right after the operation, it's swollen so it's even smaller. A teaspoon or perhaps a tablespoon of soup is all that you can eat. Some report that they can drink two cups of water a day (throughout the entire day), and some (like me) couldn't even do that for months.

For those who haven't had the operation, I would like to try to explain the feeling of fullness after eating two or three bites of food. Try to imagine a test tube about fifteen centimeters long. The tube is made of glass, and you are filling it with rice, water, a tomato, a cutlet—spoon after spoon. How long will it take you to fill the test tube? After a few spoons, the tube will be full, right? Now what would happen when the tube is completely full, and you add just a bit more?

It will simply spill out...

That's what happens after surgery. You can't eat just a bit more. Sometimes, if you concentrate, you can feel it just before you reach the limit (which means that you'll be feeling very full soon), but then again, you want to eat just a little bit more (because it smells so good and tastes great) but there's just no more room!

"Just one more bite," you think to yourself, "one last bite," but this is **the** mistake. This extra bite of food causes real pain. Sometimes it's so painful or that you have to throw up. ☹

In addition to this feeling of fullness after eating a small amount of food, you may face other challenges (I don't mean unsuccessful results of surgery, I mean common and well-known side effects), such as **nausea and loss of appetite**. A lack of appetite usually happens because the part of the stomach that controls appetite has been removed. This can last for several months and encourages weight loss. I worried a lot about it. I knew I had a few months with no appetite but was worried about the moment my healthy appetite would return.

When it did return, I was ready for the new situation because I had expected it, and my way of eating had changed completely thanks to the new habits I had learned before the operation. You can go over the list I prepared of exercises that I practiced for months before surgery, and they appear above in the chapter "Practicing the life "after" the operation "before" you go through it". I'm sure that if you do practice them, you'll be much more prepared for what lies ahead, and you'll feel much less uncertain.

Stretched skin and wrinkles – When there is such a loss in body mass, our skin doesn't shrink that quickly. As a result, facial wrinkles appear and skin may be loose on the stomach, at your inner legs, under the arms and around your neck. This depends on age and self-esteem; some feel the need to have surgery to correct this problem. Thankfully I don't feel that my skin looks terrible. I get along with my wrinkles and I'm grateful to be healthy.

Hair loss – Before my operation, I was told that the sun/hydrogen peroxide/hair color can cause hair to look dry or damaged. Today it's clear to me that the main thing that affects the hair is nutrition. About four months after the operation, my hair started to fall out, and two years later, I don't have the full head of hair I always had. The hair loss stopped, but I have no idea if this can be avoided. It's a known issue after drastic weight loss.

A constant feeling of chilliness – I never suffered from cold temperature before. I live in the Middle East, and Israel is a hot country. I always hated summer, not only because I didn't feel comfortable in a bathing suit. I always felt it was too hot, and air conditioners were my lifesavers. Since the operation, I feel cold. My fingertips are cold, my nose is freezing, sometimes the room is warm and I'm sweating; but inside me, I'm cold. This is very common after weight loss surgery, and it happens both in winter and in summer.

What does "being thin" mean?

1. Should I be admired?

How many times a day can you hear people telling you that they admire you so much but you don't understand why?

Before the operation, when I just began to hint that I was considering weight loss surgery, people kept telling me that they really admire me. I didn't feel there was anything to admire. In a way I was a loser, giving up and seeking help through the surgeon's scalpel.

After having the operation, I understood even less (and by the way, I still don't understand) what's there to admire?

Is the fact that my stomach is the size of a banana, and I can't eat very much or else I'll throw up something to admire?

I lost 22 lbs in 10 days, but it was due to the terrible nausea I experienced for two weeks after surgery—is this something to admire?

I couldn't physically eat much, so I lost more weight—is this something to admire?

I admit that it's nice to receive warm comments, but what causes people to feel this way towards major unnatural weight loss?

I asked them. When I got this kind of feedback, I asked: "Why do I deserve to be admired?"

Here are some of their answers:

"Because you made a decision and had the operation."

"Because you lost so much weight."

"Because you manage to keep up your weight loss. I know people who had the operation and gained back their weight."

"Because you look so good."

Well, thanks, but **in my opinion, there is nothing to be admired.**

I decided to have the operation because any other alternative would have led to diabetes, which runs in my family, and a serious health risk. I call that "simple logic."

I lost weight because when I didn't listen to my body after the operation and ate two more bites of food, I felt I was about to die from the pressure I felt in my esophagus. **I learned that it actually hurts to eat too much.** And I keep up my weight because I listen to my body most of the time, but I'm used to it from before. **It didn't change my eating habits after the operation, but way before as a result of practice.**

The following is a conversation I had with a friend who has undergone this operation a few years before:

We had a delicious meal together; I ate eight bites of food, and he had eighteen bites more or less (by the way, it's a very good feeling to have friends who have gone through the same experience and know how you feel), and as we mentioned the discussion above, he said:

"In my opinion, your success is the result of the balance between eating food that's good for you and physical activity...you did it."

To me, it seemed a rather strange statement, so I told him that I don't feel a success because, in the back of my mind, there is the fat lady who is afraid that all this is temporary. I feel this isn't going to last.

I feel that way because I never was able to lose weight and stay that way for very long. I never managed to stay thin for as long as I did this time. And then I said it out loud. I told him:

"I really don't feel that I succeeded. I feel that this is not going to last."

"Do you know what?" he said, "I feel that way too, and I'm five years after the operation…"

That's when it hit me that this observation of me on my life is forever.

I feel that success is a result of a long and continuous process. Not something quick and "instant." I check myself on a daily basis, sometimes even by the hour. For instance, I enjoy being able to get up and throw food into the garbage. Yes, I actually get up and throw out a sandwich or half of a sandwich that I took a few bites from or a plate of food, just because I feel I don't really want to eat it.

It took me a long time to reach the stage that I wouldn't eat food simply because I didn't really care for it, and it didn't bother me. **And this was before the operation.**

Being able to control food instead of having it control me is what I consider success.

I asked another friend that had the operation half a year before me, what's the most important thing for her three years later, and she said:

"I look carefully after the "size of my stomach" she said, "That's the most important thing in the world for me."

"The size of the new stomach" lets us, the weight lossers, feel full, which is something obese people with a gigantic stomach have a hard time feeling. It's not impossible, I guess, but it's hard to feel. Sometimes, when I was obese, I thought that I could identify fullness, but only after the operation I really felt it, and I learned to stop eating on time. When I didn't, about four or five times, I suffered terrible pain until the food "went down." I still don't always stop on time, and "time" can mean even one, two or three bites!

The attention I give my body now when eating is very different than before. I notice the taste of food, but mainly the feeling of fullness.

And that is something I agree is worth being admired for. That's the real challenge, in my opinion.

When you think of successful surgery, what do you think of? How do you measure success? Most people and perhaps you are amongst them, measure the success of this kind of surgery by the number of pounds one has lost.

If you are near surgery and find yourself focusing on the number (of pounds) or the size (of clothes) that you will have afterward, you have the wrong attitude. Running endlessly after numbers as a way of life is an impossible way to measure happiness. You look great even when the numbers don't match the measurements that you, or someone else, have decided that define good looks. If you focus on numbers, you probably won't be able to enjoy the results for a lifetime.

Assuming that most of the operated individuals lose dozens of pounds, I suggest that you **disregard this**

factor when measuring success or at least put it aside for the moment.

Most of you will lose a great amount of your weight, and then the question will be: Is success measured only by the weight you've reached? Are you sure you're happy with the many other changes you've made?

Focus on your ability to be happy and to love yourselves as a measure of success. Are you able to do that? And if not, can you understand why you shouldn't see numbers as a measure of success?

2. Shopping Spree

I was a fat little girl. Not that I was really fat, but I was bigger than the other girls my age. When you looked at me, you would say I was just a bit more than average. But if you asked me- I was fat.

When I grew up, it became part of my self-identity.

I felt inferior to other girls. It didn't matter if I was pretty, smart or talented. I was fat, and that was what counted. In elementary school it was less of an issue, but towards the sixth and seventh grades, I felt it very clearly. I associated mainly with girls of my size, my height, and my weight. That way I didn't feel so enormous compared to another classmate.

In my teen years, all I wore were black tights. That was all I had in my closet. A few pairs of black tricot pants with elastic in the waist. Sometimes I bought them, and sometimes my mother sewed them for me. I wore T-shirts and black tricot pants.

When I was in eleventh grade, I went on a diet and lost ten pounds. That's when I bought my first pair of jeans. I felt awful, **I was embarrassed to go out wearing them, but only I noticed this**. I got positive reactions from my friends; it seemed natural to them that I wore jeans…**just like everyone**. But I didn't feel comfortable. What was the thing with jeans, and what was so special with jeans on me?

Except for those jeans, there wasn't much variety in the clothes I wore. They were always big and roomy. And of course—black. During my service in the IDF army, I had to wear khaki clothes, which I hated. I hated the uniform; I hated putting my blouse inside my pants and I hated the color. But what I liked was that no matter what size I wore, the army supplied it. I could always get a new uniform in bigger sizes.

In my twenties, I went on many more diets. I gained weight, lost it, and then gained it back. And I always wore roomy and comfortable clothes. I bought my first dress at the age of 26 for my best friend's wedding, after losing weight. Of course, I gained it all back, and even more. After I got married, I went on wearing tricot clothes, big and black. I varied clothes a bit, but more or less wore the same thing. I would go into plus size clothing stores, choose black pants with elastic, and a black, red or blue T-shirt. My closet was full of more of the same clothes.

After I gave birth, I stopped wearing high heels. I was afraid I would lose my balance with a baby in my arms, and it became a habit—I switched to flat and comfortable shoes.

That's how I lived for two-thirds of my life. I was used to it. It was familiar to me.

There was a definite contrast between the way I looked and my knowledge as far as fashion, color, and design. I was always up on the newest trends: clothes, shoes, accessories, colors and jewelry—I knew what was in fashion in each season. I learned the fashion news, followed them day by day, and applied them on others. After my release from the army, I took a professional makeup course, received outstanding grades and was chosen to teach others. I then had my Bachelors in Design becoming professional in this area. This combination of talent and studies allowed me to consult others and share my knowledge. I always enjoyed helping other women look beautiful. I knew (and still know) how to match makeup to complexion, which haircut is right for what type of face, and of course, what clothes suit each person at any age. I advised women and men and guided them. But I never applied it to myself.

The change began when I joined a "non-diet approach" workshop, as part of some self awareness changes that I began to make in my life. As part of these changes I went shopping in a plus size shop and bought myself a denim jacket and a white undershirt.

The change was immediate, as well as the reactions I got from people around me.

I liked it, so gradually I added non-black clothes to my wardrobe, despite my enormous size. This was before my operation.

After my operation and the quick weight loss, I didn't have suitable clothes. I went to "my" plus sizes shop and headed straight over to size 22+ (52-54) shelves. It was ridiculous…the pants slipped down. I tried on size 18 and was satisfied to find something that didn't slip and looked good.

After a few weeks, something was wrong. The new clothes were too big, and I returned to the shop. This time, I tried on two pairs of pants: size XXL and size XL. They were both too large…so I tried on size L, which fit me perfectly.

A few months later, I was shopping one day in the mall and decided to go into a normal fashion store. I looked for size XXL but found only XL. I picked a shirt and a pair of pants and headed to the dressing room. The clothes fit me! It felt strange. I stood in front of the mirror while the saleslady looked at me.

"Do you think it looks all right?" I asked.

"Yes. You're sure it's not a little big on you?" she said.

"I don't know," I answered, "I don't really know my size." (and I heard my head go inside: "and I am not sure I know who the woman looking back at me in the mirror is…")

Two and a half years after the operation, I was still not sure about the size I was. I mean, I could guess what it is, **but that didn't mean that my brain accepted that's my size**. I still go into stores and measure the same garment in three sizes: XL, L and M.

That's what happened with my shoe size! At my peak weight, I wore a size 12 (43-44) in shoes. Today I wear size 10.5 (41). Bras, underwear, everything has changed and in a very short time!

It still confuses me; How come I fit into size L and M and even size S fits me? What do others see that I don't? How can others think that I look great, **and why don't I feel that way?**

I let the salesladies help me. Their advantage is that they see many customers and can recommend the clothes that will look good on you. **With all my sense of aesthetics and design, I couldn't cope with it on my own**, and I thank every saleslady that I met for her frankness and help. Dear saleslady, do you remember me? I'm the one that you offered a size M dress when I was about to try on a size XXL...

3. Learn to love your body

How many of you enjoy looking at themselves in the mirror every morning? Most of us don't! But, our body does so much for us, how can we hate it? This struggle with our body creates an impossible situation. We don't feel comfortable about ourselves. We always find something to blame for this feeling, whether it's cellulite in the legs, a white hair, a new wrinkle, and so on and so forth. How many times have you said these sentences?

"When I lose weight, I'll (fill in the missing words): _____ "

These are a few optional answers:

- wear tight-fitting clothes
- go for a walk/run in the park
- go bike riding, and no one will laugh at me
- have sex with my boyfriend/husband in full light
- wear large and beautiful jewelry

- wear high heeled shoes
- wear flat shoes
- wear white clothes
- wear a bikini
- go to the beach in a bathing suit

You probably have more suggestions…

(Keep on filling in the missing words): "Without being afraid of _____"

These are the common answers:

- looks
- reactions of others
- being laughed at
- being called fat
- being called ugly
- being told to lose weight right away
- being noticed
- getting stared at
- dying of shame
- being judged

All answers are correct, all combinations are possible, and most of them have nothing to do with your weight.

In day to day life, it's most likely that only you notice all the changes in your body. When you live in hope that one day things will change, you're putting your life "on hold," and you're hoping no one will notice.

Life after the operation makes you face the biggest fear many of us have: living in the present. Well, guess what? To be here, in the center of the stage, even as a thin person, can be an issue to consider.

Your body is a gift, and your happiness grants it health. After the operation, you will receive a very special gift. It has to be cared for and loved. When you accept yourself as you are, you can love not only others, you can love yourself. Wherever you are, you'll be in the center of attention. Learn to enjoy it, because it's forever.

4. Keeping your weight loss—is this the real challenge?

As part of the "social education" that weight losers experience, one of the statements you'll be told by those "who know a thing or two" will be: "It's not such a big deal to have weight loss surgery. The real challenge is to keep up your weight loss."

This statement annoys me.

First of all, it's not a matter of "competition". People have surgery for all different reasons, the most common reasons being extreme obesity and serious health problems. **Resorting to such a drastic measure is not a real test, it's a mature decision made by an adult** which causes a dramatic change in life. The real challenge is being able to survive this turnover and be happy; to accept yourselves unconditionally, as you are, and not to struggle with your weight anymore.

The main thing, in my opinion, is the inner strength that lets you look straight into people's eyes, listen patiently to what they say with the best intentions, and know that only you decide what's right for you, what's good for your body, and what you need to do in order to have a healthy mind.

I used to feel sorry for those who had weight loss surgery. I mistakenly thought that it was like giving up; I mistakenly thought that weight loss was proof that the operation was successful.

Before my operation, I never thought of asking other weight losers about their real reasons for having surgery. As a marketing consultant for designers, I always ask first of all "what is your goal?" because only after defining and understanding your goal, you can measure if you've reached it.

This is true in business, and it's true in elective surgery.

I always wondered what it would be like to be thin, and now that I'm called "thin", I truly understand that weight is not the key to happiness. Throughout the years, before and after the operation, I've met thin people with mental illnesses (anorexia and bulimia), fat people who are unhappy and people of all sizes and kinds, some satisfied with their looks and some not.

The brain is the same whether you weigh 290 pounds or 198 pounds or 165 pounds. If you don't love yourself, weight will not make a difference. I feel that living a contented and happy life and accepting who you are, with all your faults and strengths, is an important goal that can resemble the process of making drastic decisions such as divorce or weight loss surgery. Just like in a divorce that you initiate, the meaning of the decision is that **you choose** to start out on a new road in life because the previous place is simply not right for you anymore.

Every change is an opportunity to correct things and make a new start, **and the real challenge is to embrace the new reality and be able to truly love yourself!**

To what extent are you willing to expose yourself?

As you're losing a lot of weight, something else is happening that you may or may not like—you become the focus of public attention.

Try to imagine that you will lose a great deal of weight and will reach the weight you always dreamed about. Even in your wildest dreams, you never thought you would lose so much weight. You have a chin and a waist again, you're buying new clothes. Your looks have changed.

There are changes that can be seen, and there are parts of your body that you keep to yourself, and the discovery (and exposure) is yours alone.

One day I looked in the mirror, and I was alarmed…I had felt a strange lump near my waist. My heart missed a beat, and I realized I was feeling a bone that I wasn't aware of.

I examined my body and discovered that a bit higher up, there were more of these bones…for the first time in years, I felt my ribs.

The body changes so quickly that when you look in the mirror, **you don't recognize yourself.** It's hard to explain. There's quite a dissonance as far as body image, between your old body and what you see in the mirror, and how others see you. Two and a half years have gone by, and I still couldn't recognize the person I see in the mirror as myself…**I liked what I saw in the mirror, but was that really me?**

The reactions were amazing. People say I'm beautiful, and I also like what I see. I just don't seem to make the connection to myself. Because I'm fat, I've always been fat. And my mind hasn't changed, remember?

There's another aspect that affects your confused feelings. As you're trying to get used to your new self, you discover that the pounds you lost have caused a few unexpected changes: a feeling of general weakness from lack of food and vitamins, backaches (that some explain as a result of weight loss in the stomach area and change in body proportions), unstretched skin, and hair that falls out at an alarming rate. These are changes that you didn't imagine. But most weight losers experience them—all of them or only some.

Naturally, you may be upset by these changes. It seems to me that I lost a good deal of my hair. My hair changed completely after the operation. I once had a healthy and full head with hair, but as the pounds disappeared, my hair did too…

Each pound that I lost made me happy, I was grateful and told myself that even if the weight loss stopped after 60 pounds, or 90 or 110, I wouldn't complain. But it went on. **At the lowest point, I lost 126 pounds**, and I didn't like the way I looked. I wished it would stop, and when I gained a few pounds, it made me very happy.

Sounds strange, doesn't it?

I don't think so. To others it seems very strange.

The words I heard the most (besides "I really admire you" and "Is that all you eat?") were: "Are you still losing weight?" with or without adding "You lost so much weight!"

I'm sure they wanted to give me a compliment. But I didn't know what to say because I was busy feeling odd, trying to get used to myself.

My friends were so happy that I lost weight that it never crossed anyone's mind **to ask me how I felt about it**, a question that an average person in a society that idolizes thinness doesn't think of asking, and it's quite logical.

The people around me react to what they see, and according to the social ideals, apparently, I had shown a very positive example!

"You've really changed," she said. "Everyone says that you've changed. You're nicer. And more calm. And you seem happier."

That's true, I changed…I divorced not too long ago. I left a relationship that I was unhappy in. It happened a year before the operation. I felt such a relief that I began to feel much better. I felt—on a personal level, having nothing to do with my weight—that I got myself back, Limor from before the marriage. I had a successful business, and it thrilled me. I put the hard times behind me and looked ahead. You see, I was feeling wonderful even before I lost all that weight… could it be possible that it was un-noticed because of my weight?

On one hand, it's nice to receive compliments. I'm sure that your friends give you a lot of support, just like mine do, but when this happens when you're feeling very confused and in the middle of searching your identity in this massive change, here are a few to think about:

Did I look that bad before? I didn't think I looked that bad…I didn't think fat women were bad looking. Or good looking. There are some very sexy women who are quite overweight, and there are some who aren't. As for thin women, some look good and some don't. And the same goes for men. There are men who are fat and handsome, and some that are thin and sloppy.

Why are we judging people only by their looks?

Don't misunderstand me; I'm also a part of this society and these habits. I grew up idolizing beauty; I'm a designer, I'm a makeup artist, I value beauty and aesthetics, but this tendency to judge and criticize as per someone's looks is awful! That's not the way I want to live, and I don't want my children to grow up worshipping a distorted ideal of beauty.

I want to enjoy my body and let it make me happy in all ways. That's the way I felt before the operation, and I feel even more so now. I try to carefully avoid critical thoughts about myself and about judging others. It's not always easy but **like a lot of new things I adapted in my lifestyle, I have learned to adopt a different attitude in this respect.**

I hadn't realized how much my looks were of interest to others. It hit me when I saw the gap between the comments I received about my looks before and after the weight loss.

Well, you know what? That's not completely accurate. The truth is that I remember receiving very nice comments from others when I began, despite my enormous size, to change from black to colorful clothes.

If I were having the operation today, **I would begin to make intentional changes long before**. As far as eating habits, I went through a definite change, but

I wasn't prepared for other changes such as intense commenting from all around.

In addition to the eating exercises that I suggested in the chapter of "Practicing the life "after" the operation "before" you go through it" there are exercises that can help you prepare for what may, on the social level, for example, change the way you look.

Get help if necessary; take care of your appearance, **even if you haven't lost a gram**. Every change you make in the way you look before the operation will help face the reactions afterward.

Learn to listen patiently and accept people's remarks with a smile. I learned (and am still learning) important lessons about coping with the judgment and criticism of others.

I learned to literally accept every remark or suggestion given to me, and there are many of them every day. I learned that many of those remarks have nothing to do with me; they actually reflect other people's opinion and way of living.

My first time...

After a long time, a first date

The last time I went on a date was before I was married at the age of 30. I've been through so much since then—marriage, children, divorce, independence, weight that went way up and way down...and about a year after my surgery, I felt that I was ready to try dating once again.

I couldn't help thinking...will he be able to understand what I have been through? Am I ready to meet someone new if I'm not sure I really know who I am?

We met in a small neighborhood café. A nice guy is sitting in front of me, and I don't have the slightest idea what he thinks about me.

"Let's order something," one of us suggests. I wonder what I 'm doing here...a date is fine, but what am I going to eat when all I can have is four bites of food or three sips of water (and I don't mean both). What did I think I was going to do?

"I'll order wine, and you can decide what we'll eat," he offers.

I'm in a panic. What do you mean that I'll choose the food? How should I know what a nice guy usually likes to eat/wants to eat/orders?

I realized that I had no choice; I'd have to tell him that small matter about the size of my stomach. If not, I'd never get out of this.

Uhmmm…I have something to tell you," I hear myself say. He looks at me curiously (he's really nice, what a shame I have to wreck up the date with this stupid matter).

"Uhmmm…you see this salt shaker here on the table?"

He nods his head; he doesn't know what I'm leading to…

"Well, my stomach. It's as big as that, more or less…I don't know what to order, maybe you should decide…"

There, I said it.

This nice guy looks at me and gives me a big smile...

What's he smiling about?

"Mine, too," he says and goes on smiling.

Oh my god... What a surprise! What are the odds that my first date after a trillion years would be wit a guy who is also be after a weight loss surgery??

I think I like you, I thought to myself, and asked, "So what would you like to order? I eat four or five teaspoons of food, maybe you eat a little more. How do we manage in a restaurant?"

He said, "I order whatever I like, taste a few bites and leave the rest. I like good food, so I just taste a bit, that's all!"

The new experiences that your new body will lead you to are surprising and can even be funny. You might find yourself in all kinds of new situations with a date who never met you and only sees your new looks. Even sitting for dinner together or going out to a restaurant with a boyfriend, girlfriend or husband can be a completely new experience for weight losers! The portions served in restaurants, dining places and bars are way too big, especially the main course. And how do you manage at a three-course business luncheon when you can hardly finish half of the first course? Even first courses have to get your attention and new approach...

What you're facing is a process of getting to know yourself from scratch, challenging social norms and lifestyle. More and more people are having weight loss surgery, we leave half plates full, so can you imagine the confused faces of the waiters at the fine restaurants we visit?

Do I recommend surgery for weight loss?

"So, do you recommend surgery?" she asks me.

"I can't recommend the operation," I answer.

"But why not? **You look wonderful, you seem so much happier since the operation. How come you don't recommend it?**"

"I can't do that, because what you see is only one aspect of the whole process, not the whole picture. **You can't see the complete picture**; you can't imagine what I've gone through since the operation because all you **see** is me weighing 110 lbs less and dressed fashionably. I agree that what we both see looks wonderful, but these good looks are not everything.

You have no idea what goes on in my mind since the operation…I'm supposed to be the happiest woman in the world, as far as beauty and good looks, but I don't feel that way. I can't encourage someone to go into this adventure just because of social norms about looks. It's not a simple matter..."

"All right", she insists, "let's say someone is fat, and she asks you what you think about the operation. You wouldn't have an opinion?"

"No, I wouldn't. I don't really know who this person is. The fat on her body is only a small part of her. To make such a decision according to weight alone is wrong, in my opinion.

I grew up on images of runway models who participated in beauty contests, and in my work in the design and fashion world, I've met dozens of models and beautiful women, women wearing fashion clothes and professional makeup 24/7. I know all about absolute photoshopped beauty throughout the centuries, and I'm aware of this matter even more than the average woman.

Since I rarely matched this ideal, I felt I had less status, I was less smart, I was pretty—but less.

I couldn't imagine what it was like to be thin. I never imagined I would hear someone tell me what I heard today at a fashion market sale of plus size clothing. I tried on a dress that was too big on me, and the saleslady said, "What can you do, these are the problems of skinny people!" I smiled to the familiar sentence and looked around, wondering who she was talking to. It took a while until I realized that she was talking to me…but this was impossible. I am by no means those "skinny people"! You see, again, what other people see is not what I see.

So the answer is no. **I won't recommend weight loss surgery to anyone.** To those who are considering surgery, I can say that they should ask themselves if they are prepared for the challenge—for a complete and drastic change in **life habits**. I have my own personal experience regarding food, sports, day to day habits, and some of it can apply to others, are they ready for this?

We've seen that "being fat" is much more than how much you weigh or the size of your clothes. We all have an attitude and habits, and they are part of who we are. And for those who decide to have surgery, always remember that all these habits won't disappear once the operation is over, so it's a good idea to get to know the alternatives before deciding. Changing your way of life takes time, much more time than an hour and a half you get to spend in the operating room. And whether you've had the operation or you'll be having it soon, it's a good idea to think things over carefully and **practice ahead!**

Practice a different approach to eating and drinking, give up diets and dietetic food and drinks – they harm your body and soul, learn to accept yourselves the way you are, and start moving. Do it very gradually, step by step, being aware of your body that keeps you alive and lets you enjoy every moment, every day. Be the only one that chooses what is right for you.

If you haven't had the operation yet, read the book again, learn about making changes before surgery, so that you'll get there knowing better what to expect.

If you have had the operation and things are challenging, take a deep breath and take advantage of this opportunity to change old habits - old habits must change to new ones.

And if you are the caring relatives or friends of weight losers, you will also have to learn the meaning of a completely new lifestyle, with eating in particular and living in general, because your support and help make all the difference. Pass this book on to them, read it together and practice living a new lifestyle, though it may be hard in the beginning. You have the privilege of changing your attitude, feeling empathy and most important, avoiding criticism and judgment in this new situation that seems so bright and positive but takes an enormous amount of inner strength, knowledge and preparation.

My Insights of the "Non-Diet Approach" method in regards to weight loss operations

The "non-diet approach" method enables you to put an end to dieting and to the **struggle with food and overweight**. It teaches you how to eat food that you like without feelings of guilt, to love and respect the body you were born with, to lose weight and stay at a natural and stable weight forever.

The method puts an end to emotional eating (overeating with no control, snacking, compulsive eating), teaches how to listen to the body and eat according to its needs (eating when hungry and stopping when full), and how to relate to food and meals in a natural way—just as a healthy minded person does.

The state of awareness and the feeling of freedom that I developed towards food, with all my overweight and my body *before I had my operation* enabled me to truly get to know myself, my motives and my dreams, and let me control my eating in particular and my life as a whole, as I chose to.

My recommendation – with love

The guidelines that I followed and practiced and have been described in this book definitely helped me adjust to the new period after the operation. I was ready for it without even knowing how lucky I was, and preparing you for what is yet to come is my gift to you. **Knowledge is power** and it is in your hands at any point, before and even after going under surgery- learn independently, Google it, join a group near you and practice as much as possible before you go through the operation when you get to the point when you have no choice but to face reality.

An era has come to an end

This book was written during the two years after my operation and edited almost four years after. I decided to publish it when I decided to implement a session of "Promotional photos" shoot for my business, a session I had ordered half a year after my operation.

I postponed the shoot for a while when I was losing weight steadily. I asked Adi the photographer from "Adigital Studio" to wait until my weight settled down.

How did I know I reached that point? I knew that I was there when my body gained a few pounds and lost a few. These delicate waves of gaining and losing weight showed me **that I was on solid ground**. I felt that I was ready to face the camera. I admit that I was excited about the session. I think I put it off till then because I couldn't look at myself and admit that the image in the mirror was me. As long as my weight kept going down, I didn't relate with what I saw.

When things got stable, I could relax; I felt like I had returned home.

On the day of the photo shoot, I came to the studio with all my wardrobe and accessories. I wear a lot of local Israeli designer fashion, and my closet is full of designers' clothes and accessories from all over the country.

When Adi began to take the pictures, her reactions made me smile. I felt an immediate bonding with Adi and her assistant, Ayana. They both made me **feel happy, inside and out**.

I wasn't surprised. I love having photos. In the past few years, I recorded myself numerous of times in video when teaching marketing classes online (search for "Limitz" on you-tube), and I'm used to posing for the camera.

What surprised me was the result—**for the first time in two and a half years, I was able to see myself and really feel comfortable** with what I saw.

After we had finished the session, the next stages were explained to me: the photos would go through Photoshop fixes, then they would be uploaded to a common server, and I would be able to choose the ones I wanted. **At my request, Adi didn't touch the photos, and they weren't Photoshop edited**. I feel very happy with every part of me. My body and I have gone through a long journey, and I have completed a chapter of it by writing this book.

Some of the photos are on the binding of the book. The rest of them can be seen on my website:

www.NewStomacheOldBrain.co.il

For inspirational material and more on me visit me on Facebook:

https://www.facebook.com/NewStomacheOldBrain

You're welcome to visit, like and share your thoughts about the book on my Facebook page!

To designers and artists that would like advice about selling your work through the internet and on Etsy. com, you may register on my Facebook page https:// www.facebook.com/ETSY

To order my lectures, and for any other matters, I'd be happy if you write me at limitz@gmail.com

Made in the USA
Coppell, TX
12 April 2022

76395793R10079